TOO
SHARP
to
fail

This generation faces many hurdles to satisfactory employment, from saturated hiring markets to historically high living expenses. Fortunately, *Too Sharp to Fail* gives specific examples of how to develop the skillset and mindset you need to break through and build the career that you genuinely want.

—**Marshall Goldsmith**, The author of the #1 *New York Times* bestseller, *Triggers.*

Wilson uses a unique lens to share her career advice with readers. You will be caught up in her well-written story and her experience as a coach will help you ask the right questions (and find the right answers) to move forward in your own career. There is no way you can come away from this book without some excellent pointers and a large dose of inspiration.

—**Beverly Kaye**, Co-author of *Help Them Grow or Watch Them Go: Career Conversations Employees Want* and *Love It Don't Leave It: 26 Ways to Get What You Want at Work.*

This is a must read! *Too Sharp to Fail* masterfully presents the real challenges young professionals face in the workplace affecting their motivation and drive and also clearly outlines concrete steps that can be taken to rise above and accelerate your success!

—**Mignon Bissonnette**, Associate Director, Career Advisement and Pre-Professional Services, Nova Southeastern University.

It's more important now than ever before to take control of your career. In this book, Kiana Wilson uses the story of Justin, a new young employee, to guide YOU the reader through assessing and analyzing your own desires at work. Packed with practical tools and exercises, Wilson provides readers with great insights to help YOU start owning your own success. A must-read for ambitious high performers!

—**Bruce Tulgan**, Best-selling author and
founder of *Rainmaker Thinking, Inc.*

Kiana Wilson's, *Too Sharp To Fail,* is written in an engaging format that speaks to today's young professional. She uses storytelling and experiential scenarios to inform readers on how to succeed in the world of work and helps them dig into their own sense of purpose. *Too Sharp To Fail* is chock-full of practical information and tips, but offers it in such a way that allows the reader to absorb it through examples, comparisons, and real-world situations. It's a great read and a valuable resource for any young professional or those serving them.

—**Lynn Chisholm**, Director of Internships and Career
Readiness, *University of South Florida Career Services*

Kiana Wilson's *Too Sharp to Fail* offers an inspirational story with a wealth of good advice that is particularly pertinent to the millennial generation and those early in their careers.

—**Stephanie Thomason**, Associate Director of the
TECO Energy Center for Leadership &
Associate Professor of Management, *The University of Tampa*

TOO
SHARP
to
fail

How to Own
Your Career and
Thrive in the Workplace

Kiana L. Wilson

NEW YORK

NASHVILLE MELBOURNE

TOO SHARP to fail

HOW TO OWN YOUR CAREER AND THRIVE IN THE WORKPLACE

© 2017 **Kiana L. Wilson**

Published in New York, New York, by Morgan James Publishing. Morgan James and The Entrepreneurial Publisher are trademarks of Morgan James, LLC.
www.MorganJamesPublishing.com

The Morgan James Speakers Group can bring authors to your live event. For more information or to book an event visit The Morgan James Speakers Group at www.TheMorganJamesSpeakersGroup.com.

ISBN 978-1-68350-142-8 paperback
ISBN 978-1-61448-660-2 eBook
Library of Congress Control Number:
2016946881

A free eBook edition is available with the purchase of this print book.

CLEARLY PRINT YOUR NAME ABOVE IN UPPER CASE

Instructions to claim your free eBook edition:
1. Download the Shelfie app for Android or iOS
2. Write your name in **UPPER CASE** above
3. Use the Shelfie app to submit a photo
4. Download your eBook to any device

Cover Design by:
Rachel Lopez
www.r2cdesign.com

Interior Design by:
Bonnie Bushman
The Whole
Caboodle Graphic Design

Creative Writing Coach:
Dianne A. Allen, M.A.

Editor:
Anna Floit
The Peacock Quill

Morgan James
The Entrepreneurial Publisher™

Builds

with...

Habitat for Humanity®
Peninsula and
Greater Williamsburg

In an effort to support local communities, raise awareness and funds, Morgan James Publishing donates a percentage of all book sales for the life of each book to Habitat for Humanity Peninsula and Greater Williamsburg.

Get involved today! Visit
www.MorganJamesBuilds.com

Dedications

My younger self,

Today I stand in the knowledge that the career challenges I experienced for many years now serve a greater purpose. To be of service to others in this way gives me immense joy and gratitude. Never lose sight of your dreams and always have the courage to OWN your career!

To my son,

Each day I am reminded that the path to success requires a strength many people will never know. My desire for you is that this book will help you along your career journey and serve as a reminder of what is possible.

To my readers,

What may seem impossible today will one day be a distant memory. I hope the messages in this book will serve as a catalyst for you to keep pushing forward no matter what.

Contents

Acknowledgments

Friends and family, you supported me during my toughest challenges and for that I am truly grateful. Like so many others, I needed the encouragement to keep going, so thank you for not allowing me to settle. Thank you for continually putting me in situations in which I could grow and see just how amazing I truly am. Lastly, thank you for being the inspiration I needed to find my voice and become the person I knew I could be.

Mentors, coaches, and advisors, words cannot express what it has meant to receive your guidance and support over the years. In many ways, you took a chance on me by believing in my capabilities long before I did. You led me to create my own path and held my hand every step of the way. Thank you for knowing just what I needed to keep pushing forward. I will always acknowledge and be grateful for your support.

Lastly, special thanks to Danielle C. Miller, Patricia A. Sullivan, and Dr. Lashun Aron for your feedback and contributions.

Preface

Do you work for money or satisfaction? This is not a trick question. Many people believe that work is simply an exchange of service for money. And although this belief may resonate with you, I want—and need—you to understand that limiting your talents and efforts to a simple exchange undervalues and undermines who you are. As I look around, I see many opportunities for young professionals to redefine what a career can be. Long gone are the days when people started in the mailroom of a company and worked their way up the career ladder. That's simply not realistic in today's business environment. And, quite frankly, staying with one company throughout an entire career is a dated practice.

If you don't make the decision *now* to own your career, you will never realize your potential. Even worse, the chapter you're currently in will continue to repeat. Imagine your best days are behind you instead of before you. And the boss you complain about each day is as good as it gets. This could become your reality—and for many people it already is.

If you're currently happy and fulfilled in your career, then consider yourself fortunate. Although, I suspect that you too could still learn a few things. This book is for the vast majority of young professionals who want to achieve career success yet feel lost, disconnected, and directionless. The problem I see most often is that people have fallen into a routine, a rut. They go through the motions of completing tasks and assuming responsibilities without ever taking the time to understand their *who*, *what*, or *why*.

> **Who are you?** The real you. Outside of your credentials, accolades, and claims to fame. Are you the person who allow others to dictate your career by relying on their input, guidance, and direction? Are you the person who once had a voice but chose to mute it in favor of playing nice? Are you the person who comes up with great ideas but lack the courage to execute them? Or, perhaps you're the person with the guts to not only envision success but will stop at nothing to achieve it.

What do you want? You don't know? Sure you do. If you had the ability to craft your ideal career, what would it look like? Create a mental image of what you are doing every day, who are you interacting with and what the environment around you look and feel like. Now that you have this image in mind, voice your desires out loud. It may seem silly at first, but when was the last time you were this real with yourself?

Why? What is your inspiration? Why do you go to work each day? For what purpose? And don't say for a paycheck. To align yourself with companies that share your values and beliefs, you must know your *why*. More importantly, your *why* will become the driving force behind your success. It is the reason you get out of bed each morning. It is your greatest asset.

If you're having a hard time defining your *who*, *what,* and *why*, then it is likely you have resigned to a "just go with the flow" mentality—which is great for yoga, but not so much in your career. If you've been looking to other people to provide the answers, you are looking in the wrong place. Mentors are helpful for providing direction as it relates to achieving specific goals. Friends and family are appreciated for providing support and encouragement. Advisors and other related professionals are useful for planning and motivating. However, these individuals can never lead you to career fulfillment. This is up to you.

This book follows the early career journey of Justin, an ambitious, talented, and motivated twenty-something professional in corporate America. It's a short read packed with lessons that will serve as a useful reference during your early career years and beyond. As you follow Justin's journey, you will notice ideal outcomes are presented, and although your workplace interactions may differ, I want you to focus on Justin's attitude, mindset, and perspective. You see, *success begins in the mind long before it becomes a reality.* And for this reason, you will gain the most value from this book by reflecting on these areas in your career.

I know crafting a career is not easy. However, I have taken these same steps in my career, and I'm grateful for having done so. Remain open and let go of any preconceived notions. Refuse to settle for a dull, average career. My sincere desire is that by the end of this book, you will decide to passionately pursue your career with a drive and focus that inspires others. The single most important lesson I want to leave you with is that *your success starts and ends with you.* No matter what, the choice is yours. Choose to wake up from career mediocrity and choose to own your career today. You are too sharp to fail!

It's Your Career, Own It!

"Your career is a reflection of what you believe you are capable of achieving. Choose to reflect a career that inspires, motivates, and encourages you to contribute your personal best each day!"

—Kiana Wilson

········

Know Who or What
is Influencing Your Career

········

Meet Justin

Justin is smart, outgoing, and some might say, easy on the eyes. To his closest friends, he has become someone they have grown to admire over the years and see nothing but success in his future. However, Justin is convinced that people give him way more credit than he deserves. After all, he's just like everyone else his age—so he believes.

When Justin was in college, he couldn't wait until the day came when he could finally put down his textbooks and begin his career. Like many of his peers, Justin was optimistic about his future and the events that would one day lead him to great success. His vision was to graduate college, land a job in his industry, work hard, and, before too long, rise to the top of the corporate ladder.

His closest friends were much like him and in many ways shared his vision for success. Together they pushed each other to stay the course, although their professional paths couldn't have been more different. Justin—like many of his classmates—had no idea what he would major in when he entered college; he assumed he would eventually figure this out. However, he quickly learned that college was very different from high school.

Although he missed his high school friends, what he missed most was the classroom environment that dictated what he needed to accomplish each day, week, and year. Instead of counselors telling him what classes he was required to take, for the first time Justin was in a position in which all the decisions rested upon him—and the mere thought of this made him uneasy. While contemplating his choices, Justin began to reminisce on the pep talks Coach Roberts, his high school basketball coach, would give the team during his many "think long and hard about your future" speeches.

Some of you will go on to college while others will begin a career. For those with college in your sight, don't wait until you get there to start figuring out what you want to do with yourself—and if you don't know then spend time discovering that now. College is too costly of an option to pursue blindly. And for everyone in

· · · · · · · · · ·
Your career requires conditioning.
· · · · · · · · · ·

this room, remember just like in sports, *your career requires conditioning.* Take time to identify and cultivate your talents and gifts. There will be no more hand-holding once you leave high school. It'll be up to you to determine if and how you will succeed in life.

Until this point, Justin hadn't thought much about what he would do with his career. Sure, he had a few ideas but nothing concrete; and besides, he didn't have to choose a major right away. Little did Justin know, this was the beginning of a pivotal point in his education, career, and life.

During his second year in college, Justin decided to meet with his advisor to discuss options for his major. He needed to decide on something soon so he could begin to cultivate those talents and gifts that Coach Roberts often referred to. Like many college students, Justin had ideas for his major but he lacked the work experience to know if these ideas were ones he wanted to build his career around. He didn't want to risk making the wrong decision; after all, his future depended on this. After sharing these uncertainties with his advisor, Justin was directed to complete a series of career and personality assessments. The results confirmed what he already knew; he could take his pick from several majors and potentially do very well. Justin took a deep sigh. What now?

Justin and his advisor continued to discuss his interests and how well they aligned with the assessment results. After observing several classes per his advisor's recommendation Justin decided to focus his efforts on Marketing. The classes were interesting. The field was in demand. And the pay was well within Justin's expectations. This major even offered the flexibility for Justin to pursue other related careers if he later chose to go in a different direction. So, for now, he was satisfied with his choice.

Justin continued to do well throughout the following college years, yet the feeling of doubt and uncertainty grew with the start of each new semester. Sure he enjoyed his classes and was making progress toward his degree, but he couldn't escape the feeling that there might be something more out there for him. He was what some would consider a Jack of all trades. He had the aptitude and know-how to succeed in almost any area he pursued with focus and discipline. Still, something was missing.

With less than a year to go before graduation, Justin shared with his advisor that he wasn't sure if he was on the right path. For a while, he'd contemplated changing his major, but the fear of not graduating on time kept him from it. Again, his advisor directed him to complete another series of assessments. This time, however, the focus was not on his career or personality but instead, his values and beliefs. Determined to put an end to his uncertainties, Justin completed each assessment with curiosity and excitement. He was anxious to receive his results, but more importantly, he hoped the tests would confirm he had made the right choice. Justin didn't trust himself. He had changed his mind many times before and needed proof to support that he was headed in the right direction.

However, there was an even greater issue at hand. Justin wasn't simply using these external sources to weigh his options; he depended on them to dictate his decisions. Although he knew these sources could serve as great checks and balances, he never considered they could also serve as a crutch for making future decisions. This moment marked a pivotal point in Justin's life, one that could change the course of his career for many years to come.

Justin continued to have doubts but he decided to stay the course and eventually completed his degree in Marketing. A few months after graduation, Justin was offered a position with a small, family-owned marketing firm where he could put his knowledge to work. What a difference this made! Being outside the classroom helped Justin realize the root cause of his uncertainties and doubts was a lack of action. To his surprise, the more action he took in his career, the more confident he became with his decisions, and eventually his doubts and uncertainties faded altogether. For the first time, Justin was no longer living from his head—he was taking real action. What he learned most from this experience was: *clarity comes through action*—and doubts and uncertainties may simply signal a need to take action.

> **Clarity comes through action.**

Ready or Not Here I Come

Two years have passed since Justin's graduation from college and all his hard work has finally paid off. Several weeks prior, he'd landed a position with one of the city's largest marketing firms, Sky Media, and today his new journey begins.

It is 7:00 am, the alarm sounds and Justin jumps up out of bed. He's awake and nervous, yet excited as today is his first day at Sky Media. "Finally, the day has come!" he says out loud. Justin had targeted Sky Media since his senior year in college. He'd attended all of his school's career fairs, relentlessly followed the company on social media, and even volunteered with his local Marketing Association—all for the sake of gaining the experience and exposure he needed to land a role with this industry leader.

As he splashes a few drops of water on his face, he thinks about how exciting it will be to work for a large corporation. Yes, he would miss the quaint environment and close relationships he had at his old job, but he was now ready to move into the big leagues. And Sky Media was exactly the place he needed to be to start making a name for himself. After all, if he was going to reach his career goals by the age of thirty, he'd better start making a move now.

What will it be like? he thinks as he visualizes the impact he would make and the new friends he would gain. *I hope I make a good first impression.*

Justin smiles. *They have no idea they just hired their next CEO. Not only will I impress my boss with my skills but I'll also outshine and run circles around everyone there,* he thinks to himself as he looks at his reflection in the mirror.

Justin grabs a bagel and juice from the fridge and sits on his couch for a moment, taking it all in. He laughs with excitement and enthusiasm as he catches himself daydreaming about his first promotion, all the accolades he will receive, and the impact he will make within his first year. Justin hasn't left the house yet but he already has his entire career with Sky Media mapped out.

As he continues to eat breakfast, he recalls his college professor's advice, "Justin, to inspire others to follow you, you must first inspire yourself to be great." He chuckles because *great* is exactly who he will be today. Justin begins to get dressed. His previous job was much more casual, but he knows jeans and a t-shirt will not work anymore. After all, he thinks, *I'm the future CEO and I must dress to impress.* Justin grabs his pants, button-down shirt, and blue blazer. Though he doesn't think it will matter, his tattoo is hidden under his clothing—he doesn't want to take any chances on his first day at work.

Justin leaves the house and heads to his new office. While reflecting on the interviews and path that led him to this moment, he suddenly gets a sinking feeling in the pit of his stomach. Thoughts of doubt rapidly surface, one after another.

What if I can't do the job?
What if they don't like me?
What if I don't like them?

As he continues to drive, the pit in his stomach turns into knots. Justin realizes he's getting all worked up before even making it to the office, but he can't help but wonder if he will succeed or if he will be like many of his friends and eventually settle for the status quo. He laughs and dismisses these thoughts as he pulls into the company's parking garage. After taking a few deep breaths, he makes his way toward the building.

Justin arrives at the receptionist's desk where he is greeted by Julie, the administrative assistant. Julie invites him to have a seat while she notifies his manager. Justin sits patiently, wondering if she could tell how nervous he is. Then again, he thought, most people are nervous on their first day. A few minutes later, Justin is approached by a familiar face, Sean Miller, his new boss.

Meet Sean

Justin stands to shake Sean's hand. "Welcome," he says. The two exchange small talk as they wait for the elevator. Justin initially met Sean several weeks back during the interview phase. He appeared to be a fair and knowledgeable boss; someone Justin hoped he could build a great relationship with.

"Here is your desk; make yourself comfortable. I will be back shortly to introduce you to the team and give you a tour of the building." Justin sits down at his desk and smiles. He looks in the drawers, sets up his work area, and even introduces himself to his new neighbor seated in front of him. A half hour later, Sean returns with a less than enthusiastic "Are you ready?"

Sean is in his late thirties, a little overweight, and wearing a dull gray suit. His white shirt has a stain on it, and his tie looks like it has seen better days, too. Clearly, he isn't overly concerned about his appearance. Justin also notices that Sean doesn't smile much, but he isn't too worried about that. His last boss rarely smiled either, and he turned out to be a great guy.

Sean has been with Sky Media for ten years. Unlike Justin, he doesn't have a college education. He started his career with the company as a marketing intern and worked his way up.

For the last six years, he has managed a small team of five marketing assistants. He has applied for several positions with the company, but continues to get passed over. Rumor has it, he has not been very supportive of his team's efforts, and this has affected his chances for promotion.

Sean does not hide his frustrations and is often described by his employees as bitter and uninterested in their success. As a result, his team's performance has suffered over the years. He too frequently verbalizes his discontent with unpredictable rants and seems to have resigned himself to the idea that this is as good as it gets.

"This is Justin," he says as he walks past the row of desks behind his cubicle. "Justin, meet the team." Before Justin can fully introduce himself, Sean has already made his way back to the front aisle. Justin smiles at his new coworkers and quickly catches up with Sean.

As they walk through the building, Sean can't help but notice Justin's excitement. Justin raves about how great the company is and how grateful he is to finally have the opportunity to put his degree to good use. Sean listens and nods, never saying much in return. Suddenly, Sean looks at Justin and says, "Look, let me be frank with you. This company is nothing more than a paycheck, so don't get your hopes up too high. If you're lucky, you'll find a good reason to get out of bed and come here each day. Don't get me wrong; this is not a bad company, but it is far from the dream you have in your head. Look at me; after ten years of working here and being passed over for promotion after promotion, I learned to accept this place for what it is—a paycheck."

Justin isn't sure what to do or say, given that this is his new boss and he doesn't want to brush off his advice. Besides, Sean has been with the company for quite some time. *Surely he knows better than I do,* he thinks to himself. Eventually, Sean stops talking and Justin's excitement begins to turn to doubt. The remainder of the tour is much quieter.

Don't Own Other People's Experiences

Orientation

It is now 9:45 a.m. and Sean directs Justin to the training room for orientation. At this point, Justin is beginning to question whether or not he should have accepted the job. This is far from the vision he'd had earlier in the morning while getting dressed. *Was my boss right? Is this what I have to look forward to?* He thought.

As Justin listens to Greg, the representative from human resources, discuss the company's mission, history, policies, and expectations, he can't help but wonder if this is all a facade. Is the presentation a far cry from reality? At least that's the impression he got from Sean. When Greg finishes he hands out new-hire packets. Justin flips through it. Typical company paperwork: I-9, W2, direct deposit form, employee handbook, along with a list of company benefits. The rest of the morning consists of viewing company videos, introductions from department managers, obtaining system access credentials, familiarizing himself with the company's intranet, and finally, completing a few on-boarding tutorials before returning to his desk for the rest of the day.

Back at his desk, Justin reintroduces himself to his team. He learns that many of them have only been with the company for a year or less, and for the most part they like the company but have mixed feelings about Sean. The consensus among the team is that Sean rarely interacts with them, is always moody, and helps out only when he has to. The team pretty much functions without him. Justin listens as each person shares his or her experience. Admittedly, this is not what he envisioned when he accepted the job.

During lunch, Justin sits with a table of new hires from his orientation class. One by one each person at the table shares his or her background, work experience, and details about their new position. As the discussion develops, the conversation turns to Greg's presentation. However, Justin can't help but think about what his team had shared with him. Is he the only one with a boss like Sean? The others seemed to have nothing but good things to say about their bosses. *What am I going to do? There's no way I can achieve my goals without Sean's support*, he worries.

As Justin walks to the parking garage at the end of the day, there is a sense of satisfaction in knowing he got through day one. His new coworkers seem to like him, and he is much more at ease after spending time with them. However, he wonders what day two will be like. Sean's words play over and over in his mind as he heads home. *This is the place where dreams die. If you're lucky, you'll find a way to cope and get through the day. Otherwise, you won't last long here.*

Settling In

It's day two and Justin arrives early again. Admittedly, he doesn't have the same pep in his step as he did the previous day, but he is still optimistic and ready to get started. He's looking forward to seeing what this day of orientation and training will bring. As he drops his belongings off at his desk, his boss Sean waves good morning. He seems more positive today. Justin quickly grabs his tablet and heads to the training room. Greg has already arrived and is greeting everybody as Justin sits down.

The day's agenda is written on the white board, and a packet of information sits on the table in front of him. On the outside of the envelope are the words *Your Roadmap to Success*. Justin immediately perks up as he makes himself comfortable and begins to read through the documents. One by one, Greg discusses each document and even references several employees who followed the outlined career development process and have since achieved great success with the company. Justin thinks, *Finally, information I can use.* Justin begins to feel hopeful; perhaps his research was accurate and Sky Media is a great company after all.

Suddenly Justin's eyes are drawn to a document entitled *New Hire Mentorship Program.* As Justin reads through the information, he wonders whether he should take advantage of this opportunity. The program seems like a great way to learn more about the company and to get a jump-start on advancing to the next level. However, he already has a lot of learning to do in his new position and doesn't want the mentorship program to interfere with his timeline. Justin has no intentions of staying in an entry-level role for long, and according to his plans he will be in a new role in less than a year's time.

Since the program requires manager approval, Justin decides to get feedback from Sean before making a decision. Later that afternoon, Justin approaches Sean to discuss the program. As he explains his interest, he begins to notice Sean's lack of attention as he fumbles through papers and periodically glances at his emails. "What do you think, should I sign up?" Justin asks. Sean shrugs his shoulders and says, "Look, if you want my approval, just give me the form." After a few seconds of hesitation, Justin hands it over and Sean signs off.

As Justin stands up to leave, Sean warns: "Like everything else in this company, the program looks good on paper—but don't be fooled, this is just another program to get people all worked up for nothing. No one ever benefits from these programs. They are only in place to make the company look good." He waves Justin away.

During lunch, Justin drops off the paperwork to human resources and doesn't give his conversation with Sean a second thought; he wants to check out the program for himself. After all, *success leaves clues*—he recalls from a business class he took in college. And he's ready to find these clues for himself.

> **Success leaves clues.**

Later that week, Justin receives an email from Maria, a senior leader in the company and the mentor assigned to work with him. Unlike Sean, Maria's email is warm and welcoming. Within the first two lines she congratulates Justin on taking the most important step of his career and states how excited she is to work with him. The email ends with several questions for Justin to answer in preparation for their first meeting. Justin looks over Maria's questions and carefully gives each one considerable thought before responding.

Question One: Why did you sign up for a mentor?

"I signed up for this program out of curiosity. I heard about the value of having a mentor in college but never actually had one and was interested in learning more about it." *Besides*, he thinks to himself, *I doubt Sean would ever have the willingness to take me under his wing.*

Question Two: What are your career goals?

Over the next several minutes, Justin gives the question some serious thought. *What are my career goals?* he repeats to himself and answers: "I want a career that is reflective of who I am. One that makes me happy and provides a sense of purpose and meaning. A career where I can fully utilize my knowledge and skills. And I want to learn as much as I can and quickly move up in the company."

Question Three: What do you hope to accomplish by the end of this program and why?

"I would like more clarity and direction regarding my career path. At times, I think I know what I want, but I have no idea how to get there. I want to give myself every opportunity to be successful here and signing up for this program is the first step. What I want to walk away with are the tools and resources I need to drive my career forward."

Meet Maria

Justin arrives a little early for his meeting with Maria. The meeting room is empty and he isn't quite sure what to expect. He has no real idea what a mentor does or how the program works, but he wants to be successful, so he shows up with an open and optimistic attitude. Up until this point, Maria was just a name on his computer screen. The door opens and in walks a woman with an air of confidence about her and a big, friendly smile. She welcomes Justin and reiterates her excitement to work with him.

Maria leads the conversation, covering the duration and requirements of the program along with what Justin can expect to receive from her as his mentor. She pauses throughout to see if Justin has any questions for her, but he is so consumed with the opportunity to work with Maria that he simply nods in agreement and allows her to continue.

During the conversation, Maria shares that she has been in the marketing industry for approximately ten years and with the company for a little over six years. She started with Sky Media in a role similar to Justin's, only she worked for consumer marketing rather than content marketing. Maria goes on to discuss how the company allows her to grow and advance her career in ways she hadn't imagined when she began. She uses lingo such as "being empowered," "taking ownership," and "making a difference."

Justin is inspired by his conversation with Maria. It's much different than the one he had with Sean. Maria and Justin share the common goal of success, and he recognizes that having her, the Director of Consumer Engagement, as his mentor is an absolute advantage for his career.

The interaction between Justin and Maria is like a conversation between old friends; there is a sense of comfort and familiarity between the two of them. They take turns sharing their backgrounds and what led them to this point. Maria discusses how she began in the mentoring program. "When I first started with Sky Media, I was much like you, Justin. I had a lot of goals, ambition, and drive, but I had very little direction on how to navigate the corporate world."

Maria goes on to talk about the lack of support she received from her boss and how frustrated and disengaged she had become with each passing day. Justin locks into her every word, relating to everything she says.

"One day I approached my boss with the idea of working with other leaders in the company to gain more exposure. Anne, my boss at the time, looked at me and replied that my idea would be a waste of company time. For me, this was a cry for help since I had already begun to consider a job elsewhere, but to my boss it was nothing more than a far-fetched idea."

"It was at that moment when I decided to be courageous. I realized I had a choice to make. Would I continue to ignore how unhappy I had become or would I take decisive action and change my career experiences? After all, I wasn't quite ready to leave the company; I just wanted the opportunity to expand my skills. As you might have guessed, I chose to stay," she finishes.

Maria continued to detail the path she took to get her ideas in front of anyone who would listen. This was her career and she refused to place her success in someone else's hands. Through her hard work and suggestions, the new hire mentorship program was developed a year later, and who better to lead this new initiative than Maria herself. Justin smiles and nods. He knows Maria is just the person he needs to help jump-start his new career.

Maria shifts the conversation to the email she received from Justin. "I read your responses to my initial questions and I believe you have made a great decision. Our time together will be centered on helping you gain better clarity around your career goals, determine how to best develop your career capabilities, and position you to be successful here. But before we delve into those areas, I would like to learn more about you. Tell me more about yourself, Justin," she asks curiously.

Justin glances down at the table. Before he can respond she says, "Justin, who you are is essential to the work we will do together. There are two types of people in this world: those whose career is an extension of their identity, and those whose identity is an extension of their career. The difference is *when your career is an extension of your identity, it becomes an extension of who you are.* Give this some thought and be prepared to discuss next time."

> When your career is an extension of your identity, it becomes an extension of who you are.

Justin stares appreciatively at Maria. He wishes Maria could be his boss. She loves the company, has achieved a great amount of success, and is already challenging him. She's given him exactly what he needs most: leadership support. For Justin, it seems like Maria understands him and wants to see him succeed. And for Maria, Justin represents the young go-getter she was when she began her career. *To be young, optimistic, and driven—there is no better feeling in the world*, she thinks to herself as she shakes Justin's hand and exits the room.

·········

Develop and Expand
Your Career Capabilities

·········

The Journey Begins

After Justin's meeting with Maria, he walks to his desk, grinning from cheek to cheek. He's excited to be working with her for the next ninety days. He's even more excited about the possibilities that lie ahead for him. Upon returning, Justin walks past Sean's desk.

"So, how was your mentor meeting?" Sean asks.

"It was great! We discussed the program requirements, expectations, and even talked about my career goals. Maria, my mentor, is very encouraging," Justin replies.

"There you go with all that career mumbo-jumbo talk. You'll see; I'm your best bet at happiness in this place. Mark my words, you'll end up like the rest of us. Anyway, glad I could help out," Sean says sarcastically before turning his attention back to the stack of paperwork on his desk.

Over the next few days, Justin continues to think about Maria, her comments, and the inspiration he received from their meeting. This reinforces some of his decisions to work for Sky Media in the first place. *Could I move up as fast as Maria?* he wonders to himself as he answers emails and attends to his work. Justin trusts Maria as a leader and knows she supports him, so he gives his full attention and commitment to their mentoring relationship.

By the end of the first month of mentoring, Maria and Justin had built a level of trust and rapport that he didn't have with his boss or any of his coworkers. In fact, Justin has never had such a powerful and influential relationship in his career. Somehow, Maria understands him on a deeper level, and Justin is always more inspired after talking with her. His confidence, drive, and focus on his goals has increased immensely, and he's starting to view his career in a new light. He knows he is better for having chosen the mentorship program and is even more grateful that Maria is his mentor.

Justin also notices that others hired before him seem to be in a rut and have resigned to settling for the status quo. He never hears them talk about their goals or about moving up in the company. In fact, many of them complain daily and seem to lack any sense of meaning or purpose in their work. They say very little and do just enough to get through the day. Justin is determined not to end up like them. He continues to follow Maria's guidance and often refers to her career positioning questions to ensure he remains on track.

• • • • • • • • • • • • • • • • • •

1. What skills or talents do you bring to the table?
2. How does this align with your career goals?
3. What value does this provide the company?
4. Why should the company invest in you?
5. What do you need to be successful here?

• • • • • • • • • • • • • • • • • •

Decision Time

After the second month of mentoring, Justin discovers he's developing a clearer vision for his career, one he did not have prior to working for Sky Media—at least not to this extent. This new awareness is a source of motivation for Justin as his vision continues to take shape with each passing day. He is thankful he made the decision to accelerate his career by participating in the mentoring program early on. Even though he has to work harder and answer tough questions, he can already see the results of his efforts as compared to others who are simply buying time. Justin wants to be on the fast track to success and is willing to work for it. He can feel his inner fire burning. *Could this be what passion feels like?*

Most of the mentoring program challenges Justin to focus on strengthening his knowledge and skills. Halfway into their second month of mentoring, Maria starts to notice a change is Justin's enthusiasm. She asks him about this change and Justin replies, "I'm still unsure what value I bring to the company. I have followed all of your guidance but I just don't know." Maria nods and pauses for a moment. She then asks Justin whether he has received any feedback from his boss. Justin shakes his head and says, "He barely talks to me, and to be honest, I don't think he even cares about my goals."

Maria reminds Justin of what he wanted to accomplish from the mentorship program. "You told me that after this program ends, you want to have the tools you need to drive your career forward." Justin nods his head. Maria continues, "I can direct you to the tools and resources you need to be successful here, but it is up to you to take action." Justin appears puzzled. He has done everything Maria has suggested since beginning the program. *This must be another one of her lessons*, he thinks.

"You see, Justin, to know the value you bring, you must ask for and expect regular feedback from those you work with and for. It's through this feedback that you will gain the most insight," she said. Maria and Justin then proceed with discussing how he can best approach his boss, along with the importance of maintaining a career development plan to be used during his meetings with Sean.

. . . .

**Ask for
and expect
regular
feedback.**

. . . .

"Lastly, there may come a point in your career when you must manage up. What I mean by this is, you may have to teach your boss how he or she can best assist you to succeed. Taking action in this way will require guts, but remember, you should always be the driver of your career," Maria emphasizes. Justin has never considered either of these before but is more than grateful for Maria's guidance and reassurance.

The following week, Sean approaches Justin's desk. "We need to talk," he says. Justin is confused by Sean's sudden willingness to talk, but follows him into his office and closes the door behind him. Since beginning at Sky Media, Justin could count on one hand the number of times he and Sean have had a discussion, let alone exchanged any type of communication.

Sean begins to rant about how he's been watching Justin and has noticed how different he is compared to the rest of the team. "This place is nothing but a dead end, and you are working like you are actually going somewhere," he whines. "Well, I'll tell ya, them days are gone. No more climbing the corporate ladder. It is just a made up story to get dreamers like you to comply and work harder for less. Your only focus right now should be meeting your performance goals. I want to help you make it, but you have to tell Maria you no longer have the time to participate in the program. Besides, there is more than enough work to keep you busy without wasting your time with her."

Justin swallows hard and keeps quiet, not knowing what to say. He's gained a lot from Maria's guidance and direction and certainly doesn't want to quit the program. Sean tells him to give his future with Sky Media some thought and focus on what's important today. Sean then waves his hand, dismissing Justin away. Justin breathes deeply and returns to his desk. For a few minutes, he lets his mind wander as he contemplates his next move. Although Maria has been extremely helpful to him, he doesn't want to disappoint his boss.

Why is he so negative? Maybe he has talents he is not using and is resentful of my progress, Justin thinks to himself. After a few minutes of pondering his dilemma, he begins to review the notes from his meetings with Maria, then takes a few minutes to observe his coworkers and where he stands in relation to them. During his short time at Sky Media, he was already outperforming the rest of the team. Not only was he effective in his role, but he has an upbeat attitude and a very different outlook on his career than the others have on theirs. *There's no way I'm going to be like them*, he thinks. And with that thought, he chooses to stay in the program.

Moving Along

Maria and Justin's next meeting starts with Maria turning the floor over to Justin and asking if he has any questions or comments. He answers, "Why is it that some individuals in this company care about growth and career development while others only care about meeting performance goals?" Maria smiles and asks him to explain. Justin goes on to share his most recent interaction with Sean and how he thinks the two of them are complete opposites. Maria listens and validates his concerns, as she too had experienced this in her career. She reminds him there are many people in a large company and their agendas may differ. Some people are only concerned with themselves and looking good in front of others, while there are others who understand the benefits of collaboration and developing others.

"Remaining focused on your goals in the midst of uncertainty will prove to be your greatest asset," she tells Justin.

This response, though sincere, makes him feel much less at ease. *Do I have what it takes to succeed in this kind of environment? How can I learn to deal with people who don't share my vision for success? Will there always be a Sean who I will have to deal with?* he wonders.

As Justin works day in and day out, he can't help but notice the vast difference in the attitudes and behaviors of those around him, from his coworkers to the managers and even to those in senior leadership. Some people greet him with a smile and appear genuinely helpful, while others rarely make eye contact and act as though he doesn't exist. Maria helps Justin to understand this better by talking to him about each person's belief system. She points out that some people believe that individual efforts alone will lead to career success and rarely lend a helping hand. Unfortunately, they just don't understand the value of building healthy workplace relationships. She then quotes the African proverb: "If you want to go fast, go alone. If you want to go far, go together." Justin wants to go far—very far—and he is beginning to see the power of understanding himself as well as the motivations of others. Maria explains that often people who are rigid and difficult to work with are gripped by some form of fear, with the fear of success being the most difficult fear to overcome.

"Justin, are you afraid of success?" asks Maria. Justin thinks for a minute and responds with a resounding, "No, absolutely not! I am driven to be successful." He then goes on to explain his desire to be satisfied and fulfilled in his career and to have a deeper meaning of success than just accolades and money. Justin wants to be known as a good leader, one who knows and understands the goals of his team and cares for their welfare. He knows Maria is the perfect mentor because she is compassionate and driven, but not at the expense of others.

·········

Your Attitude Determines
Your Outcome

·········

Happiness

Entering the final weeks of the program, Justin is more comfortable talking about his inner world and what motivates him to achieve success. He is excelling in his position and even begins to assume additional responsibilities. His confidence and focus are strong, and his vision is sharp.

One Friday afternoon, Sean approaches Justin's desk and asks to speak with him in a nearby conference room. As

Justin enters the room, his eyes are immediately drawn to a folder Sean places on the table. The serious look on Sean's face causes Justin to wonder what they're going to discuss, and he takes a seat.

"I received the results of the team's 360° feedback survey and it appears that on average, the team is not happy with my leadership. So, I'm meeting with each person today to gather more information as to how I can improve in this area." Justin isn't sure what to say as he is caught completely off guard. He wants to be honest with Sean about his experiences but is hesitant to do so. After all, this is his boss. He wonders if Sean is really open to receiving feedback or if he has other motives?

"Well, you're not around much to help and when you are, you seem disinterested."

"Go on," says Sean.

"It's not like I'm complaining or anything, but I would like to receive more direction and support from you. In my last job, I had a really good relationship with my boss, but since I've been here, it seems like you only take an interest in me when I'm making you look good."

Justin pauses for a moment.

"Did I just say that out loud? What I mean is …"

Sean interrupts, "I know what you mean, and you're right. I haven't shown much interest lately."

Justin's heart sinks for a brief moment as he listens further to Sean. "Justin, I have been watching you since your first day and the progress you've made has been remarkable, given the lack of support I have shown. Even so, you continue to remain positive and have been a great example for the team. It is rare for someone as focused and driven as you to hang around this place for long. I'm sure you've discovered that this place can be a beast at times and if you're not careful, it will turn you into someone you barely recognize."

Justin wonders where this is going as Sean continues, "I have to admit I was surprised you continued to take advantage of the mentoring program even after I suggested you quit. Your actions showed me you had the guts to stay the course and not get deterred by my personal views. I can't tell you the number of times I've seen talented people like yourself give up on their goals simply because they didn't have the courage to own them. Justin, I owe you an apology. I have not been the best example of a leader to you."

Justin's eyes grow big as he listens to Sean. "You remind me a lot of myself when I first started my career. Believe it or not, I wasn't always this way. I had goals and aspirations too, but somehow I lost them along the way. I guess you can say I relied too much on other people's opinion about what I should do with my career. I eventually got to a point where I didn't know what I wanted anymore, and I no longer recognized the person I'd become. Not only did I stop accomplishing the goals I'd set for myself, but even worse, I didn't care. My career was no longer my own, and I accepted this as my fate."

"Your spark and energy have been refreshing, Justin. Because of you, I'm starting to rediscover my purpose for remaining here so long. It's not that I gave up completely on my career or my team for that matter. I simply lost sight of my *why* many years ago and it wasn't until I hired this young show-off a few months ago that I was reminded of this. You see, long before I ever took on a leadership role, I knew I wanted to be a leader."

"Why so?" Justin asks.

"Because I realized that leaders have the ability to bring out greatness in others and I wanted to be in a position to do just that. I imagined leading a team in which my greatest claim to fame was not in the numbers my team produced but the people I developed along the way. Justin, your attitude and actions have inspired me to be a better leader. At the rate you're going, you may one day lead this entire place! I suppose I did pretty well hiring you after all!" Sean chuckles as he gathers up his papers and heads toward the door.

Justin sits for a few more minutes thinking about this change in Sean and what might have prompted it. It can't be just about the feedback results; surely he's received similar feedback in the past. Why change now? There had to be a catch. Justin's meeting with Maria was the next day, so he decides to save this conversation for their time together. Reflecting on Sean's comments and the progress he's made, Justin realizes how on target he is to reaching his goals.

Getting Back to Business

The following day, Justin shares his gratitude with Maria for helping him overcome the initial challenges he experienced with Sean and also for leading him to define his *who, what,* and *why.* Maria acknowledges the great progress Justin had made and even points out a few observations of her own. After several minutes of catching up, Maria asks Justin if he knows how long they have been working together. He thinks she is quizzing him.

"Um, almost three months, I believe," Justin replies. Maria nods her head and says that to get the most out of their final weeks together, she wants to ensure he has a game plan in place so he can continue to make progress on his own. Maria gives Justin an assignment to complete before their next meeting. The assignment seems straightforward, but Justin knows Maria always has a great lesson for him in each of her assignments, and this time was no different.

• • • • • • • • • • • • • • • • • •

Assignment:
1. Detail your career vision for the next two years.
2. What obstacles or challenges do you foresee?
3. What skills do you need to gain or develop?
4. Who might you seek for support?
5. How will you measure your progress?

• • • • • • • • • • • • • • • • • •

Justin leaves the meeting motivated and ready to address these questions, but before doing so he reviews his notes:

Who are you? I am an ambitious person who enjoys tasks in which I can interact and collaborate with others through creative forms of expression. I am flexible and open to growth and success and will not impose limitations on my potential. I am not mediocre; I am exceptional. And although I have yet to attain the title of a leader, I perform like one each day.

What do you want? I want a career with a company where I can use my creativity each day to influence others and make a positive social impact. I want an environment that is flexible, inspiring, and supportive. I want to do work that I am not only good at but enjoy. Most importantly, I want to do work that matters.

Why? I am inspired to do work that contributes to the greater good of society. This is when I feel most accomplished.

In reviewing his responses, Justin begins to see a long-term plan developing. He came to Sky Media thinking he would one day become CEO and retire. Now, he sees that he must remain open and flexible as his career continues to unfold. After all, there are more opportunities both within and outside the company than he initially imagined.

Maria's Goodbye

With less than a week remaining in the program, Maria emails Justin and asks him to meet her for lunch on Friday, and he agrees. As Justin walks into the employee café, he sees Maria sitting at a table in the corner with a woman he doesn't know. Maria smiles and signals for him to come over. Not knowing who the woman is, Justin walks over confidently. He is sure to make a great first impression. *After all*, he thinks, *I am on my way to the top and I must look and act the part!* As Justin approaches the table, Maria introduces Justin to Lisa Daniels and tells him she's asked Lisa to join them for the beginning of their time together for a specific reason. Justin shakes Lisa's hand and sits down.

Maria tells Justin that Lisa is a career development coach with a specialty in working with high-potential employees. Maria goes on to explain that Lisa is an independent coach with whom the company has contracted to assist with the development of emerging leaders.

"I asked her here today because I believe you are a great candidate for our leadership development program." Justin sits quietly. His legs begin to twitch with excitement. Maria continues, "The program requires a referral from a senior leader and if you agree, I will complete the paperwork this week." A huge smile covers Justin's face and without hesitation he nods with excitement. "How can I turn that down?" he exclaims. "Thank you for considering me."

"Lisa," Maria says, "Justin is a talented, focused, and driven young man who has what it takes to go as far as he wants in his career. He has experienced a few challenges here, but as you know, that is all part of the journey. He has remained focused on his goals and has completed each assignment I gave him with eagerness and curiosity. This young man is a great asset to the company, and with your support he will crush his career goals in no time."

Justin is temporarily taken back by Maria's kind words. Lisa smiles and turns to Justin and says, "If you choose to have a great career, I am the woman who will get you there." Lisa shares a little about her experience in corporate America and her motivation for helping young professionals, which is the reason Sky Media hired her as a coach. Justin is surprised by the similarities they share.

The conversation continues for a few more minutes before Lisa stands up, shakes Justin's hand, and says, "I look forward to working with you soon." She then excuses herself. Maria and Justin are now at the table alone.

For the remainder of their lunch, they discuss Justin's options for further development. Justin has many questions. "What exactly is coaching?" he asks Maria. "Coaching is where two or more people partner in a collaborative process to support, inspire, and maximize personal and professional growth." Maria goes on to explain how she too has a coach, and although she is a leader in the company, she still looks forward to achieving far more in her career. Justin is impressed. In the last ninety days, Maria has become a trusted advisor, and Justin has grown to rely on her encouragement, even when he questions or struggles with clarity.

Justin and Maria review his career development plan and discuss his overall growth during their time together. Maria remains focused on Justin's long-term goals and keeping his momentum going. Lastly, Maria stresses to Justin the importance of seeking new and creative opportunities to contribute in his

> **You can't always focus on moving up.**

current role. "You can't always focus on moving up. There is much to be gained through expanding and enriching your current responsibilities."

Justin tells Maria how happy he is that he made the decision to enter the mentorship program and that he is grateful for her willingness to guide and support his career success. "Whether I continue my career here or go elsewhere, I will never resign myself to career mediocrity. I don't know what the future holds for me, but I know I'm courageous enough to find out!"

Maria smiles and high-fives Justin. She then shares that being his mentor and helping him accelerate his career has been rewarding for her as well. She urges him to check in with her from time to time and let her know how he's doing. "And as you continue to grow in your success, remember that your greatest accomplishments will be gained through your service to others," she says. They shake hands and part ways. It's a bittersweet moment for both Maria and Justin.

·········

Take Time to Reflect and Assess Your Development

·········

Meet Coach Lisa

S everal weeks after his lunch meeting with Maria and Lisa, Justin receives an email from Lisa stating that Maria's referral for him to participate in the leadership development program was approved. She tells him she's also received a copy of his performance review and the notes Maria had saved from their meetings. Lisa mentions that she is looking forward to working with him and asks him to complete the attached forms before their first session.

Justin opens up the documents one by one. The first document is a coaching agreement form that outlines the parameters of their relationship. It covers confidentiality, expectations, accountability, and the overall coaching process. The next document is a questionnaire about goals, vision, accomplishments, strengths, and challenges. Lastly, an assessment is included to gauge Justin's level of professional happiness. *Wow*, he thinks, *this really goes deeper.* Although he has become accustomed to answering questions from working with Maria, he can't help but notice the depth of Lisa's questions, which challenge him even more. *I think I just might enjoy this coaching stuff!* Justin laughs out loud while picturing what the next level of success will look like for him.

As he completes the forms, he begins to wonder why there are so many personal questions, but he continues. He gives careful thought to each of his answers and returns the forms to Lisa, as instructed.

When Justin arrives at his meeting with Lisa he is excited and talking faster than usual. He slows himself down and focuses on Lisa's inquiries. Justin is anxious for her to take the lead since he isn't sure how coaching works. Lisa reviews Justin's questionnaire with him and they discuss each of his responses in greater detail. She frequently asks for him to elaborate and appears to be genuinely curious. Justin notices and admires these qualities. Lisa displays a deeper level of listening than he is accustomed to. It is apparent that she is interested in what he has to share. She summarizes, questions, and restates what she hears during their conversations. Experiencing this during their first session reassures Justin that he's heading in the right direction, and this puts him at ease.

"As your coach, I will provide guidance and support to assist you with developing your career capabilities and achieving both short and long-term goals. You are responsible for letting me know your goals and agenda for each session, and together we will work to accomplish them. Our journey together is like going on a trip; you give me the destination, and we will construct the roadmap together. There may be some ups and downs, changes in direction, or unexpected setbacks along the way, but remember, there is more than one way to reach your destination!"

As Lisa is talking, Justin thinks about Maria and tries not to compare them, but he can't help but do so. He realizes how important his work with Maria was and the value he gained toward getting his career off the ground. He wonders how coaching will compare. While Lisa continues to explain the coaching process, Justin can't help but notice her strength and authority. Lisa is direct in her responses and never accepts anything less than her clients' best efforts. At the same time, she is warm and easy to talk to. Justin can see her commitment and dedication and is happy to be working with someone who will hold him accountable for his actions—or lack thereof.

Lisa continues to ask a lot of questions. At times, Justin knows the answers and at other times a long, awkward silence fills the room. Nevertheless, Lisa encourages Justin to take his time and think through his responses. A half hour into the session, Justin starts to relax even more and begins to enjoy their interaction. The biggest difference he notices between Lisa and Maria is that Lisa does very little talking during their time. In fact, she insists that Justin does the majority of it. Only when Justin needs guidance will she offer it, and only with his permission to do so. Lisa is impressed by Justin's openness to each question, and it is clear to Justin that Lisa is taking a genuine interest in helping him achieve his goals.

Lisa reassures Justin that she has no agenda for him and simply wants to get to know him better by understanding the motives and intentions that underpin his words and actions. She goes on to say that self-awareness and personal mastery are vital to a long, successful career. Justin smiles as she speaks; he likes what he is hearing. "You don't make as many misjudgments when you know yourself," Lisa tells him.

By the end of their session, Justin is amazed by the progress they made. They've identified some resistance he has toward change and discussed his environment and the importance of creating winnable outcomes. They also tackled a few limiting beliefs and assumptions he holds about the workplace and his ability to thrive. Before departing, Justin reflects on their time together and recaps his takeaways. He even comes up with several actions to be taken before their next session. Justin thanks Lisa for her time and heads back to his desk.

Winning Environments

Shortly after returning to his desk, Justin can feel the obvious negativity around him. His coworkers are complaining about work, management, and anything and everything as long as there is someone to listen and agree. Justin, however, is tired of the negativity. Although he is naturally optimistic, the pessimistic attitudes of his coworkers are starting to wear him down. *If they don't want to be here, then why don't they leave*, he thinks. Justin is not going to let the negativity and pessimism get to him. Not today. So he pops his headphones in his ears to block out the chatter.

Before Justin can get settled, Matt, a coworker who sits across from Justin, comes to his desk and asks to speak with him. Justin locks his computer and the two of them head to the break room. Justin knows it must be serious because Matt mostly keeps to himself and rarely talks to anyone on the team, let alone him. Matt shares that he is thinking about quitting. He is fed up with the team's dynamics and feels like he is just buying time until the inevitable happens—either he quits or gets fired.

Matt explains that although Sean had made some improvements and is more visible to the team, he is still not receiving the guidance and support he needs. Matt wants to know Justin's secret. "You," he begins, "seem to be adjusting just fine here, and I need to know how you have been able to last this long without completely losing your mind!" Justin listens but isn't sure he can be much help. "I mean … " Matt hesitates for a few seconds … "How have you managed to maintain a positive outlook?"

"Oh, that's simple."

"Really?" Matt says, thinking out loud.

Justin continues, "Both my mentor and coach have taught me several lessons about creating a winning environment. I am more than happy to share them with you." Matt shrugs his shoulders and Justin begins.

Lesson 1: Your environment always win.
You will never succeed in an environment that is not designed to support your success. If a supportive environment does not currently exist, then you will need to either create it with the help of a mentor, coach, or trusted advisor or you will need to find an environment that better lends itself to your success.

Lesson 2: Develop an attitude for success.

Your attitude will determine your outcome. If you have an attitude of settling and not caring, it will reflect in your work and level of commitment. The right attitude will take you far, and the wrong attitude will keep you where you are.

Lesson 3: Stand out.

Conformity has and will always be a success killer. You can never be successful fitting into someone else's design for your career. Differentiate yourself by staying true to who you are and the skills that you are uniquely positioned to offer.

Lesson 4: Network internally.

Much of your success will depend on your ability to acquire workplace champions. These are your raving fans. They are the leaders and decision makers who support and promote your efforts without you knowing. They have your back and want nothing more than to see you succeed.

Lesson 5: Take action early and often.

Never be afraid to act. It is through action that courage and confidence grows. Those who act either achieve success or learn how to be successful going forward. Either way, failure to take action will never lead to success.

After his conversation with Justin, Matt feels a sense of hope and agrees to consider what Justin shared with him. He thanks Justin and the two of them return to their desks. Prior to this conversation, Justin had never given much thought to the impact he might have on those around him. And, just like that, it sinks in. He is no longer Justin, the new guy in marketing. He is someone who his coworkers have grown to respect and admire. In fact, Justin has become the change he once sought. *Now that's growth,* he thinks as he chuckles quietly to himself.

Thinking back on the initial challenges he experienced, it is clear that by shifting his attitude, mindset, and perspective, he can redesign his environment, and more importantly, he now has a better understanding of the value he brings to the company.

Personal Mastery

Justin often stops by a local coffee shop near his apartment when he needs quiet time to reflect on his career. He finds that the warm and upbeat atmosphere of the quaint little shop is the perfect place for him to focus on his thoughts and goals. Over the past ten months, Justin has thought a lot about his experiences at Sky Media. Dealing with negative people, avoiding distractions, and overcoming setbacks and challenges were all part of a typical week.

As Justin makes himself comfortable at his favorite table, he slowly sips his latte and reflects on how much he has grown and changed. He pulls out his tablet and jots down his thoughts. He's gotten in the habit of doing this on a regular basis thanks to his work with Lisa. She's encouraged him to take note of any thoughts, feelings, or other areas of awareness that might surface in between their sessions.

While people-watching and journaling, Justin decides to look at some of his earlier entries. He is curious to know just how much his mindset and perspective have shifted. He smiles as he reads notes from his mentorship days. Maria knew the right questions to ask to get him thinking about how he wanted to "show up" in the workplace. The "Who am I?" question will be answered much differently now, he realizes.

Journal Entries

I am so glad I have chosen to be proactive in my career instead of whining and complaining all day like many of my coworkers. It's like they have given up and are content with being unhappy. Not me!

I have better control over my thoughts and actions today. While everyone else chose to react negatively to the new company changes that were announced, I chose to remain flexible, adaptable, and open-minded.

I couldn't do that before. Thanks to Maria, I reminded myself that distractions from others can be seductive, yet they need not lure me away. I can stay focused on my goals. She always knows what to say to get me back on track.

I see so many possibilities for myself and being stuck is not one of them. I choose to not view my career as something I have to tolerate in order to pay my bills and survive. Viewing my career in that way would indicate a strong misalignment between who I am and the career I am pursuing.

This coaching stuff is pretty cool and Lisa has helped me to grow in ways I never imagined. She never tells me what to do. Instead, she encourages me to use my best judgment, while reminding me that it's okay to make mistakes. Being able to reflect on my mistakes and use them to move my career forward is something that I could not do before.

I am in charge of my career, and I trust my decisions. Although the guidance and support that I received from Maria, Lisa, and the others has been beneficial, I will always use my inner knowing to guide my actions.

As Justin continues to reflect, his attention is drawn to a memo where he listed his initial goals prior to working with Lisa. He is shocked and somewhat embarrassed by what he had written. Sure, he had several goals listed including making strong workplace connections, assuming more responsibilities, and building his professional network, but what he quickly realizes is that each of these goals only scratched the surface of his potential. In fact, he hadn't realized until now that he had placed limitations on his success. He remembers having once heard, "Success begins in the mind long before it becomes a reality." It's clear to Justin that based on the goals listed, he hadn't imagined much success for himself at the time.

> "Success begins in the mind long before it becomes a reality."

Determined to put into motion a plan that would ensure he takes bigger risks in the future, Justin begins to tweak his career development goals. However, this time his focus isn't on easily attainable goals. Instead, Justin allows himself to think big. Really big! Justin knows that if he wants to win big he has to risk big, and the biggest risk to his career success lies within the confines of his mind. After adding the final touches to his revised plan, Justin journals:

My greatest challenge and inspiration is pushing past self-imposed limitations. Although this may not be an easy feat, I am satisfied in knowing that today I at least made an attempt. Personal mastery is achieved one day at a time.

Looking Ahead

Justin wants no part of average and with the help of his support system, he continues to stretch himself outside of his comfort zone. Although this process isn't easy, he continues to recognize its importance. Justin smiles as he thinks back to the days of being stretched so far that he became frustrated, overwhelmed, and even briefly considered giving up. *It's funny how things that once challenged me, I now do with joy and ease. I see things from a different perspective now.*

Taking advantage of mentoring and coaching has allowed Justin to experience success in ways he never imagined possible, and as a result, he is not the same person. In fact, Justin has not been the same person for quite some time. It wasn't until today, however, that he realized this journey wasn't just about his career, it was about who he'd become in the process.

Justin has strategically positioned himself for success by demonstrating the desire, focus, and teachability that is vital to moving his career forward. Although he has had struggles and challenges like everyone else, the biggest difference is the attitude he has when approaching his career and the lessons it has offered him thus far. Justin knows that his career reflects his belief in his capabilities, and he sees himself as capable. Whenever he has doubt or fear, he utilizes his coach and trusted advisors to remind him of his goals and focus.

Average workers are passive bystanders in their careers. However, Justin remains inspired each day to take steps to develop his career, and he chooses not to let the actions or opinions of others dictate his success. Justin has learned to effectively navigate the corporate environment by having the right attitude, mindset, and perspective. This kind of disciplined thinking has catapulted his success. Some of the biggest lessons he carries with him each day are: (1) Take time for reflection; (2) Stay true to who you are; (3) Never let anyone dictate your career; and (4) Take action early and often.

> **Average workers are passive bystanders in their careers.**

Therein lies the keys to your success! Justin is too sharp to fail, and so are you!

Afterword

When I first envisioned this book, I thought of it simply as a short story from which my readers could gain a lot of value. My hope was that readers would not only read my book (let's face it, many books are started and never completed), but would also use it as a guide and reflection tool to achieve greater career success. However, in the process of writing this book, I not only grew personally and professionally, but I also gained a new awareness about the importance of taking action and pushing past one's limiting beliefs and fears. In other words,

I am not the same person I was when I started this journey, and I plan to keep growing and changing.

In many ways, Justin's workplace experiences were my own as a young professional. In fact, I have since learned the workplace experiences presented in this book are shared by many people, both those who are new to the workplace and those who have more years under their belts. When discussing these topics with others, the feedback I typically received from more experienced professionals was that they wish they had known these lessons earlier in their careers. To be honest, I wish I had known them earlier in my career, too. On the surface they may appear simple to grasp and implement, but in reality, these lessons can be challenging, especially in workplaces where the culture does not support growth and personal development.

If you are a more experienced worker, you may have learned some of the lessons presented in the book through trial and error. After all, most college courses don't emphasize the soft/interpersonal skills needed for career success. If your experiences were similar to mine or the many other professionals who have shared their journeys with me, you know it isn't easy to learn how to effectively navigate the workplace in this way.

Although Justin's journey has ended, your career journey may just be starting or may need a few tweaks. This book will certainly get you started. However, what I realized upon the completion of Justin's story was that although there were some great lessons shared throughout, I want to make sure you understand the value of professional coaching, as I believe it is often overlooked and underutilized, and should be incorporated in every stage of your career development.

To give you more insight into this area, I decided to add another section to the book titled "Coach Me." Throughout my journey of writing this book, I learned that I still struggle in many ways with developing my career; however, the guidance and support I continue to receive from my coach has been invaluable.

Coach ME!

"You can't push anyone up the ladder unless he is willing to climb."

—Andrew Carnegie

This section contains career-related coaching excerpts along with thought-provoking questions that will assist you in addressing each of these areas in your own career. Grab a pen and paper or a voice recorder and allow me to be your coach. Note: Client names and personally identifiable information have been changed to ensure confidentiality.

Grow ME

Kelsey has been at her job for two years now. When she initially accepted the position, her desires were simply to learn as much as she could and let the work she did guide the course of her career. In fact, she felt pretty lucky to have obtained a "good job" so early in her career. During Kelsey's day-to-day activities, she has learned a lot about what it takes to be successful in her role. However, she's always had a desire to do more, learn more, and be more. Although she has approached her boss with these concerns, the response she received was not supportive. In a nutshell, she was told, "We could all use someone to develop us but the bottom line is if you truly want to grow in this company, you will have to do it yourself. You can't depend on anyone else to do it for you." This response simply confirmed Kelsey's belief that no one ever took the time to develop her boss, and as a result, she has no idea how to develop others. How frustrating!

Coach ME

Coach: Based on what you shared, it appears you are unhappy with the development support you have received from your boss and despite addressing this with her, there has been no resolution. Is this correct?

Kelsey: Yes.

Coach: Let's discuss.

1. **What exactly are your career development goals?** It's important that you are clear about this before reaching out to others for assistance. Those who are willing to assist you and are in a position to make the greatest impact will expect you to have already given this some thought, and you want to make sure you are prepared. Don't overthink this! Your plan does not have to be formal and can be for your eyes only. It's simply a tool you will use to manage and track your progress.

2. **What resources have you utilized within the scope of your role to grow and develop your career (i.e., tuition reimbursement, workshops, job shadowing, cross-training, etc.)?** When discussing your development needs with others, it's always more beneficial to demonstrate that you have already been proactive in your efforts and are at a point where you desire additional guidance. Typically, if you have not been proactive then you may receive a canned response of "there are many resources available to employees; have you signed up for any workshops, online training, etc.?" You do not want to be perceived as lazy. So you must do the heavy lifting first before reaching out to others.

3. **Besides your boss, who else in the company (influencer) is aware of your desire to grow and**

contribute more? Your boss may not always be the best person to assist you with achieving goals. Yes, you should share this information with him or her, but you should not solely rely on their efforts. You want as many influencers as possible to champion and assist you. If you are not sure where to begin: (1) Start by creating a list of the people in your company who embody the qualities and characteristics that you admire, lead the area(s) you are most interested in learning about, or have a large network and can introduce you to key influencers. (2) Set the intention to reach out to these individuals to learn more about them, their respective area and what needs they may have. (3) Be sincere in your interactions and efforts and always seek to add value. The more influential champions you have, the more likely you are to receive the support you need.

4. **What external resources are available to assist you with achieving your professional development goals?** Expanding on the previous question, you should also identify several external resources. Specifically, think about individuals in your community, professional circles, church, etc., that, given their professional status, work ethic, reputation, knowledge, experience, or connections, can serve as a mentor or guide to you. You want to be strategic about the alliances you form so

take the time to understand their value before soliciting their support. This is not the time to wing it!

Also, consider professional associations related to your area(s) of interest. Typically, these associations are dedicated to assisting professionals with growing and advancing their careers. They provide ample opportunities to expand your knowledge and grow your network. Consider perusing their industry-related articles, attending a webinar or workshop, or perhaps getting involved with their local initiatives.

5. **What limitations do you carry that could prevent you from taking proactive steps towards your professional development goals?** Fear, uncertainty, and doubt are usually the big ones that pop up. No one is exempt from these. Yes, I know that stretching yourself and taking action in a new way can feel uncomfortable and at times it may even scare the heck out of you. No worries, this is all part of the process. So take a moment to think about the counterproductive attitudes, thoughts, behaviors and beliefs that you carry. I want you to get out of your own way. To do so, you must first understand what's blocking you from powerfully moving forward.

6. **What would you like to be held accountable for regarding your development and how will you**

ensure commitment? Take some time to think about this. After all, you don't want to be perceived as a talker instead of a doer. So make sure you are challenging yourself enough to ensure you are being held accountable for making steady progress. Examples may include: Pay for a workshop in advance, commit to contributing to a major project at work, or sign up to lead a company initiative that will entail acquiring new knowledge and skills. It's up to you to determine the amount and kind of motivation you need.

Connect ME

Josh is new to his company. In another week he'll hit the six-month mark, and for the most part he enjoys his role. Outside of his colleague Jay, who sits right next to him, he has not developed any other work relationships and is concerned that this could impact his advancement. Although he considers himself a people person, he's been hesitant about forming new relationships. In previous jobs, this was never an issue. However, Josh is unsure whether he will be with the company for the long haul, and instead of putting forth the time and energy to make new connections, he'd rather keep to himself for now. As a result, he's become withdrawn and it's starting to impact his overall attitude and perception of the company. He realizes his desire to connect is important, but what's the point in doing so if he's only going to be with the company for a short while?

Coach ME

Coach: Let's jump right into what you've shared. You mentioned a need to connect. However, you are hesitant about doing so at this time. Help me to better understand what you are experiencing.

Josh: Okay.

1. **Why is it important for you to connect in the workplace? Specifically, what does this do for you?** Think about your need to connect with others. Is it simply to make gains in your career, or is it much deeper? Does connecting with others energize you? Does it provide a sense of belonging or acceptance? Take time to explore your desire to connect and why this is a concern. Doing so may provide insight about your needs and how to ensure you are in a position to thrive.

2. **What benefits will you gain from forming new relationships?** It's important to understand what's in it for you. Is it to exchange value? Combine efforts? Or even perhaps to demonstrate your skills and capabilities in a more visible way? Whatever the reason, you must

be clear on the expected benefits. Otherwise, you may not see the value in making new connections.

3. **In what ways would you like to connect with others?** Answers may vary depending on the person, but some examples are: eating lunch with others, joining committees, or participating in company activities. In some cases, connecting with others may satisfy your need for healthy dialogue. While in other cases, you may enjoy working together and being a part of a team. Take some time to think about what forms of connection would be most beneficial to you and why.

4. **Why haven't you put forth the effort to connect with others? What's really holding you back?** This question can be a real eye opener! Think about the thoughts that are surfacing. Do you carry any limiting beliefs about yourself or others? Have you previously experienced a negative reaction when connecting with others in the workplace? Is trust an issue? It's far too easy to say, "I'm not sure how long I'll be with the company," but the even bigger challenge is addressing why this matters in the first place. Also, think about how this same theme may show up in other areas of your life besides the workplace. How do you typically connect with others in general? Be honest with yourself.

5. **Imagine the kinds of relationships you most desire in the workplace. What do they look like and how can you begin to build them?** Think about everyone you interact with on a daily or weekly basis. Include your boss, coworkers, parking attendants, the receptionist, etc. What relationships, if any, do you desire to have with these people? What ownership are you willing to take in regard to establishing and developing these connections? What actions do you want to commit to taking and when? Again, this is up to you to determine—but understand that without action, change can never take place. So, don't procrastinate.

Motivate ME

Carlie has noticed that over the last several months she is becoming more and more disengaged at her job. She can't figure out what is causing her to feel this way, but it has led to her doing the bare minimum just to meet her performance goals and keep her job. In the meantime, she has submitted her resume to several companies in the hope that she could eventually leave altogether. Carlie has expressed that she watches the clock all day, has become snappy with her coworkers, and dreads the thought of being there each day. She has mentioned her frustrations to her coworkers, but beyond that she mostly keeps her feelings to herself. As long as she meets her goals, no one questions her commitment. However, what bothers her the most is that it seems as though no one cares about how unhappy she has become. Should she continue to buy time until something else comes along, or is there another solution?

Coach ME

Coach: If I understand you correctly, you are no longer motivated at work. When did this begin?

Carlie: It started several months ago. I'm not sure what happened; one day I just realized I didn't like my job.

Coach: Let's explore.

1. **Thinking about the events that led to this realization. Were there any patterns or contributing factors?** Identifying the triggers that may have led to your sense of unhappiness, frustration, lack of motivation, etc., can help you determine how to best address this situation. For example, you may feel stuck in your current role, need greater challenges, or perhaps you hold beliefs or expectations about where you should be in your career as opposed to where you actually are. All of these things and more can lead to workplace disengagement and a lack of job satisfaction.

2. **What is your primary source of motivation in the workplace?** It's necessary to first understand what

impacts your motivation before you can address a perceived lack in this area. Maybe you're motivated by a job well done, receiving recognition from your boss, or perhaps a nice bonus check. Knowing and understanding what motivates you is important to understanding how you perceive yourself in relation to your career. If what drives and motivates you is lacking or nonexistent in your workplace, then this may signal a need for change. Change can be in the form of a new role, new or expanded responsibilities, or perhaps a shift in your perspective. There's no right or wrong answer here. This question is all about gaining self-awareness.

3. **What are you seeking to gain through motivation?** This question is not about material or monetary gains but about what motivation provides for you on a deeper level. In other words, do you feel more empowered, accepted, worthy, or accomplished? We often operate in a state of not knowing the true impact of our desires. So, if your desire is for more motivation, why? Take time to pause here and reflect.

4. **Are your expectations realistic?** This question typically raises a few eyebrows. Unrealistic expectations can often lead to a lack of motivation. Watching the clock, contributing at minimal levels, snapping, disengaging, and even detaching yourself from others can all be the

result of expectations that are not in alignment with your perception of how things should be or could be. If this is the case, consider adjusting them accordingly.

5. **Why haven't you shared these concerns with your boss?** Do not underestimate the power of your voice. I know you may be reluctant to share your concerns out of fear of retaliation, or perhaps you don't want to be perceived as being whiny or difficult. Instead, you complain to your friends and coworkers in the hope that another job opportunity will come your way soon. Know this: your workplace experiences are a result of *your* actions or lack thereof. If you have not shared your concerns with your boss then you are missing out on a great opportunity to receive the guidance and support you desire. Although jumping ship may seem like a good idea, in many cases it's a temporary fix instead of a long-term solution.

> Your workplace experiences are a result of *your* actions or lack thereof.

Appreciate ME

Vanessa has always done well at her job. In fact, she far surpasses her coworkers and has even taken the liberty of informally training her colleagues when needed. Although this has been very satisfying to her thus far, she is starting to feel undervalued.

To gain more visibility, she has asked to participate in new projects and has even inquired about taking on more duties. Her boss knows what a great employee she is and has stated that he can't afford to lose her. However, at this time there are no opportunities available to expand her role on the team. Vanessa simply does not understand this. She has done everything she can to contribute at optimal levels, yet no one seems to appreciate her enough to acknowledge her value in a way that will help to advance her career.

Coach ME

Coach: What you seek most right now is to be acknowledged and valued in proportion to the level of effort and commitment you are putting forth. Is this correct?

Vanessa: Yes. It's like they expect me to continue making them look good without ever having to acknowledge or support me or my goals. I'm just tired of it all.

Coach: I see.

1. **In what ways would you like to be acknowledged or appreciated?** If you are unable to answer this question then pause for a while and do not proceed without addressing it. There are great resources on the market that can assist you with determining your workplace preferences. Your preferences may be tied to

your values, personality, culture, etc. After you have identified your preferences for being acknowledged and appreciated, determine whether they are feasible within your company. Areas you should consider include the company's culture, workplace practices, organizational values, and the list goes on. Don't shortchange yourself, do the work!

2. **How can you best communicate your concerns to your boss**? Your boss may not know or understand how you feel, so you must ensure that you are proactive in your efforts. You can't assume that just because someone is in a position of authority or leadership they have all the answers. Your boss is not a mind reader, and making incorrect assumptions can negatively impact your career progression. Determine the best way to address this situation, and initiate the conversation accordingly.

3. **Have you ever felt appreciated**? In some cases, this may lead to a long line of questions. For example, if you previously felt appreciated, what has changed? If you've never felt appreciated, why is this a concern now? Though this question may be simple on the surface, the deeper meanings behind it may reveal far more about you than initially anticipated. Take your time here.

4. **Are your actions reflective of the acknowledgment or appreciation you desire?** I know this is a loaded question, but for good reason. People typically express themselves in the way they expect others to reciprocate. Almost like a mirror, it reflects what is being presented. It's the same with you. In what ways do you acknowledge or appreciate yourself and others around you? Although this may seem like I'm pointing the finger at you, I'm not. However, I do want you to be more aware of your actions. What I have learned from experience is that when I begin to express dissatisfaction, someone will usually shift the focus to me and whether or not I'm demonstrating the things that I desire. So, don't be afraid to put a mirror up to yourself. You may discover some interesting truths.

Hear ME

Dylan is a big thinker and he often comes up with ideas he believes will impact the overall success of his company. Although he is currently in an entry-level role, he has his sights set on quickly moving up the career ladder and takes every opportunity to showcase his abilities. During his downtime, Dylan enjoys strategizing about how he and his coworkers can be more productive, operate more efficiently, and crush their monthly sales goals. Even though he may not have the title of a company leader, he's always thinking like one! The problem, however, is that Dylan believes his voice is not being heard in a way that truly makes a difference. Sure, his ideas are acknowledged, but rarely are they implemented. He is beginning to feel like his manager doesn't trust his ideas and lacks confidence in his overall abilities. From his perspective, she and the other leaders just don't get it. Dylan is growing more frustrated with each passing day, and questions his future with the company.

Coach ME

Coach: You want your voice to be heard in a way that fully acknowledges your capabilities and allows you to contribute in a more meaningful way. Is this correct?

Dylan: Yes, and I'm tired of making suggestions that are shot down without a justifiable reason. I may not have ten or twenty years of experience, but I work hard on researching and coming up with good strategies that I believe would benefit the entire company—if someone would just listen, really listen. I'm sorry; I'm just frustrated and these people just don't get it!

Coach: I can certainly hear your frustration.

1. **Why is it so important for you to be heard?** Depending on the specifics of your company (i.e., size, culture, structure, etc.), you can feel as though you're losing more and more of yourself with each passing day.

If this rings true for you, take the time to first explore why your voice matters to *you*. Understanding the *why* behind this is the first step toward identifying how to effectively move forward. Your *why* may stem from wanting to prove yourself, eagerness to demonstrate your value, or perhaps you just want to feel that your voice matters—that *you* matter.

Regardless of your *why*, it's essential that you take the time to explore the cause of your frustrations as this can reveal powerful insights. Be open to the possibility that your desire to be heard may be a result of a belief or assumption you hold. Also, make a mental note of any feelings or emotions that may surface as you think about your workplace experiences. Doing this will help to uncover the root of your desire.

2. **In what ways do you want your voice to matter?** It's not just about being heard. You want your voice to matter in a meaningful way. Now that you've taken the time to explore the *why* behind your desire, let's move on to what this looks like. Create a visual picture of this in your mind. In what ways is your voice being heard? Are you regularly sitting down with your boss and discussing your thoughts and ideas? Are you leading or greatly contributing to team meetings? Are you empowered to make autonomous decisions? You get

the idea. Give this some real thought and remember, as I stated earlier in the book, "Success begins in the mind long before it becomes a reality." The vision you create will serve as a guide for determining actionable steps toward achieving your desired outcomes. One final suggestion: be honest with yourself and create the vision that you truly desire—whether you believe it is achievable or not at this point.

3. **Can your ideas be presented in a better way? And if so, how?** It's easy to point the finger at others when you feel you are not being heard. However, effective communication is not one-sided. It requires you to do some introspective work and determine how to communicate in a way that others are receptive to. Think about how you communicate with others on a day-to-day basis. Do you just ramble off ideas at random times, hoping that others will understand the value in them? Do you present sound justification or reasoning for your ideas? Do you consider the goals of the team or company before presenting your ideas? As you can see, it's not just a matter of coming up with an idea, communicating it, and then expecting it to be immediately implemented. There is work that needs to be done on your part to ensure you are speaking the

language of your boss and the leaders of your company. Always think in terms of adding value.

Strengthen Your CAREER Muscle™

"The best way to predict the future is to create it."
—Abraham Lincoln

The following section is designed to jump-start and maximize your career development efforts. You may choose to complete each document in its entirety or focus specifically on those areas that support your current career needs.

Note: The suggested time frame for the conditioning exercises can be adjusted to fit the culture of your workplace and be repeated as needed.

Career Positioning Worksheet

Instructions: Please complete this worksheet to the best of your knowledge. Don't overthink your responses or base them on what you have been conditioned to believe about yourself or your career. Silence the head chatter, and remember, this is all about you!

*The Career Positioning Worksheet can also be downloaded from www.ASharperU.com/Resources.

Description of terms:

G.A.I.L.: What **G**remlins (negative self-talk or inner critic), **A**ssumptions (beliefs accepted as true without proof), **I**nterpretations (opinions or judgments based on one's understanding), and **L**imiting beliefs (acceptance of a belief that limit or inhibit action) do you carry about your career?

Focus: What do you desire the most at this stage in your career? Where would you like to focus your initial career efforts?

Passions: What do you enjoy or love to do? What are you doing when you're the happiest? Are there any recurring patterns of interests, hobbies, etc.?

Metrics: How do you measure success in your career? What guidelines, standards, or parameters do you use to assess whether you have successfully completed a career milestone or initiative?

Motivations: What energizes you? What gets you fired up to contribute at optimal levels?

Sharpness: What sets you apart from others? Think about the unique qualities, attributes, gifts, strengths, and values that you possess.

Skills: What specific skills do you possess? What comes easily to you? What areas do others consistently compliment you on or request your assistance? Your skills can either be hard skills (i.e., graphic design, writing, etc.) or soft skills (i.e., listening, communicating, critical thinking, etc.) or perhaps a combination of both.

Values: What are your most important values? These are your non-negotiables. What morals, principles, behaviors, etc., are important to you? Your values shape your decisions and are reflected in your actions.

Vision: How do you see your career progressing within the next 1–3 years? This includes your goals, aspirations, and desires. What are you doing in your career? Describe this in as much detail as needed.

Vision	
Values	
Motivations	
Passions	
Skills	
Sharpness	
Metrics	
Focus	

Tame your gremlins!
What are the top three gremlins
you have regarding your career?

Assume nothing!
What assumptions have you made regarding
the achievement of your career goals?

Validate interpretations!
What opinions, viewpoints, or judgments do
you carry about the success of your career?

Say NO to limiting beliefs!
What limiting beliefs do you have about your career?

Career Conditioning Exercises

• • • • • • • • • • • • • • • • •

Lesson 1: Clarity comes through action.

Message: Uncertainty and doubt stem from a lack of action.

Question: What thoughts or ideas have you not taken action on that can make a big impact in your career?

Conditioning: Over the next fourteen days, commit to taking action on one of these areas, even if you are unclear about the results.

Goal: Get moving and stop living from the comforts of your head.

• • • • • • • • • • • • • • • • •

• • • • • • • • • • • • • • • • •

Lesson 2: Use external sources sparingly.

Message: The biggest mistake you can make is to rely on external influences to dictate your career.

Question: What areas of your career have you relied on external sources for guidance instead of trusting your judgment?

Conditioning: During the next twenty-one days, commit to strengthening your gut by trusting and depending on your inner knowing capacity to assist you during the decision-making process. Make note of what you discover about yourself.

Goal: Break free from dependency habits.

• • • • • • • • • • • • • • • • • •

• • • • • • • • • • • • • • • • • •

Lesson 3: Everyone has the capacity and capability to lead themselves.

Message: To lead others, you must be able to influence them. However, to lead yourself, you simply need to decide to do so.

Question: Are you taking the leading role in your career?

Conditioning: For the next two weeks, commit to observing and making note of all the areas of your career in which you are not taking a leading role. Discuss these areas with a trusted advisor and resolve to address them within the next sixty days.

Goal: Gain awareness of where you may be falling short as the CEO and leader of YOU incorporated.

• • • • • • • • • • • • • • • • • •

• • • • • • • • • • • • • • • • • • •

Lesson 4: Never take ownership of someone else's beliefs about your career.

Message: Don't let others cloud your career vision by dumping their insecurities or shortcomings on you. Your career is not based on someone else's opinion of what they believe you are capable of achieving. The only opinion that matters is yours.

Question: Have any of your career goals changed due to someone else's feedback or advice?

Conditioning: Reflect on a career-related goal that you dismissed largely due to someone else's opinion. Make a decision today to revisit this goal and decide for yourself if it's worth pursuing. If it is, commit to taking one action each week toward achieving it.

Goal: Never lose the courage to see your vision through to the end.

• • • • • • • • • • • • • • • • • • •

• • • • • • • • • • • • • • • • • • •

Lesson 5: Your perspective will determine your outcome.

Message: There will always be those who are unhappy and may even take great joy in recruiting you to jump on their bandwagon. Don't fall for this trap; form your own opinions.

Question: What perspectives do you carry about the people you work with and the environment you work in?

Conditioning: Do your own research and then enlist the assistance of others to either confirm or dispel the accuracy of your point of view.

Goal: Do not allow others to influence or dictate your perspective.

• • • • • • • • • • • • • • • • •

• • • • • • • • • • • • • • • • •

Lesson 6: Grow and develop your career capabilities.

Message: Don't miss out on essential opportunities to develop your career. Take advantage of every resource you currently have at your disposal.

Question: What career-related resources have you failed to take advantage of, either within or outside of your company?

Conditioning: Within the next thirty days, learn more about the opportunities that exist in your company and commit to taking advantage of at least one new resource to further the development of your career.

Goal: Leverage career and professional development resources.

. . . .

. . . .

Lesson 7: You are not your career.

Message: Many people lose themselves in their careers and have no understanding of who they are outside of them.

Question: Is your career an extension of your identity? Or is your identity an extension of your career?

Conditioning: Take time to reflect on who you are, what you value, and the beliefs you hold regarding your career, and determine if the work you do is an extension of these areas.

Goal: Create more alignment and synergy in your career.

. . . .

. . . .

Lesson 8: Positon your career for success.

Message: There's power in knowing the value that you bring to your company and how this can best be leveraged to meet the needs of both you and your organization.

Question: Is your career positioned for success?

Conditioning: Review the career positioning questions that Maria posed to Justin on page 24. Make note of your responses and commit to sharing them with your boss or another trusted advisor.

Goal: Initiate career conversations with those that are in a position to support your success.

• • • • • • • • • • • • • • • • • •

• • • • • • • • • • • • • • • • • •

Lesson 9: Feedback is imperative to career success.

Message: Don't assume that feedback will automatically be given.

Question: When was the last time you received constructive feedback from your boss that was not part of a formal review process?

Conditioning: Within the next thirty days, commit to scheduling time with your boss to discuss the strengths that he or she has observed as it relates to your work, interaction with the team, and your future with the company.

Goal: Get in the habit of asking for feedback on a regular basis.

• • • • • • • • • • • • • • • • • •

● ● ● ● ● ● ● ● ● ● ● ● ● ● ● ● ●

Lesson 10: You will not go far alone.

Message: Seek ways to collaborate and contribute to the success of others.

Question: Are there any teams, committees, or projects you can assist with?

Conditioning: Research opportunities to get more involved in your organization outside of your immediate role, team, or department. Commit to participating in a new activity before your next performance review.

Goal: Increase your visibility and build new relationships.

● ● ● ● ● ● ● ● ● ● ● ● ● ● ● ● ●

● ● ● ● ● ● ● ● ● ● ● ● ● ● ● ● ●

Lesson 11: Strategically exiting to advance your career.

Message: There may come a time when your employer no longer serves your career needs. Acknowledge this and have the courage to seek new career opportunities elsewhere.

Question: How will you know when it's time to make a strategic exit from your organization?

Conditioning: Review your career vision and note any areas where you may need to seek new opportunities elsewhere in order to reach your goals. *Do not* jump ship! For now, just be aware of these areas and discuss them with a trusted advisor.

Goal: Assess your career viability with your current employer.

· · · · · · · · · · · · · · · · · ·

· · · · · · · · · · · · · · · · · ·

Lesson 12: Workplace champions are necessary for career success.

Message: Your ability to acquire champions (influential leaders) in the workplace who can attest to your knowledge, skills, and abilities will prove to be an invaluable tool.

Question: Which individuals in your workplace could potentially serve as champions for your success?

Conditioning: Within the next thirty days, commit to having a conversation with at least one of the champions you identified. Share your career goals and offer to assist them in an area that demonstrates your strengths and capabilities.

Goal: Build strong workplace support systems.

· · · · · · · · · · · · · · · · · ·

••••••••••••••••••

Lesson 13: Up is not the only way to go.

Message: Career expansion (i.e., expanding in your current role by assuming additional tasks and responsibilities) is one of the best moves you can make toward achieving your goals.

Question: What opportunities exist in your current role to expand your skills and capabilities?

Conditioning: Within the next ninety days, commit to taking action on at least one career expansion opportunity that aligns with your career goals. There are many ways you can accomplish this. Some examples include: assisting with special projects, cross-training in a new function, or completing a job rotation assignment.

Goal: Identify lateral opportunities for career growth.

••••••••••••••••••

••••••••••••••••••

Lesson 14: Your beliefs will influence your actions and your actions will determine your success.

Message: Limiting beliefs are those beliefs you carry about yourself, your abilities, or even how you believe others perceive you. There is likely no factual basis for these beliefs, and if left unaddressed they can and will prevent you from achieving career success.

Question: What limiting beliefs do you carry about your career? Examples may include: *I'm not smart enough; I'll never achieve my goals; No one will ever believe in me.*

Conditioning: Counter each limiting belief you identified above by creating new beliefs in support of your career success. Each time a limiting belief surfaces, commit to taking a specific action of your choosing, to replace them with thoughts that affirm your success.

Goal: Identify and eliminate self-imposed barriers to career success.

• • • • • • • • • • • • • • • • • •

• • • • • • • • • • • • • • • • • •

Lesson 15: Your environment always win.

Message: You will gradually adapt to your environment over time whether you choose to or not. The key to winning is creating environments that support your success.

Question: Are there opportunities in your current environment that you can leverage to create winnable outcomes?

Conditioning: Make note of these opportunities and discuss them with your boss or a trusted advisor. If applicable, add them to your career development plan. **Goal:** Create safe and supportive environments.

• • • • • • • • • • • • • • • • • •

What IFs

Clarity

What if ... I don't know my *who*, *what*, or *why*?

There are many resources you can use to gain clarity. However, I must first warn you, *do not* rely solely on external means to find these answers. Doing so will take you down a road of dependency and frustration instead of gaining the insight and awareness you seek. It is more difficult to break free from this dependency than it is to simply trust and utilize your internal compass to guide you. Some of the resources I've used in the past were: career assessments, journaling, meditation and self-reflection, self-help books, and workshops. All of these may be useful to you. However, the point I want to stress is that while there are a plethora of options out there, use them sparingly and only as a means to support your journey, not drive it.

What if ... I don't know what my career goals are?

Mentoring and coaching are great options to consider even if you are unsure of your career goals. In fact, the best time to take advantage of these resources is during the career exploration stage. Although some mentors may use coaching skills to assist their mentees, mentoring (in the context it is used in this book) is geared toward providing the professional development tools and resources you will need to be successful in the workplace, whereas coaching focuses on setting goals and achieving specific outcomes. Goals can be anything from gaining more clarity in different areas of your career to working toward the achievement of a specific outcome.

The Workplace

What if ... my company does not have a career development process in place?

It is your responsibility to ensure you are receiving the support and resources you need to be successful. If there is not a process in place to assist you then: (1) Outline your career goals, current challenges, and any other areas of interest or concern. (2) Schedule a meeting with your boss to discuss this information and make sure you are clear on your expectations. (3) Make note of how you would like to be held accountable, including the frequency of progress check-ins.

Do not be passive and wait until your performance review to discuss career development. Instead, schedule meetings with your boss in advance to discuss next steps. You will have to own and manage this process on a regular basis.

What if... I work for an unsupportive boss?

You cannot control whether or not you receive support from your boss, but you can control how you approach this situation: (1) Be clear on what you need. (2) Discuss your concerns with your boss and let him or her know how much you would value their support. (3) Highlight any areas you have observed where you can assume more responsibility to assist the team and your boss. (4) Seek alternative ways of gaining the support you need from other resources, either internally or externally.

What if... I work in a toxic environment?

Toxic workplaces are more common than you might think. Remember, your environment always wins, and you will never flourish and grow under these conditions. If you are not in a position to remove yourself from a toxic environment, put as much space between you and the negativity as you can. Buy time until you're able to strategically exit.

Mentorship

What if ... I'm not sure that mentoring is right for me?

Mentoring does not have to be a formal process. If you are unsure about working with a mentor, reach out to someone who you value and commit to working together for an agreed upon time in a mentor-mentee capacity. Give this process your best effort and then determine whether you want to continue the relationship.

What if ... my company does not have a mentorship program?

If a formal mentorship program is not available, identify several people in the company early on who you believe can add value to your career growth. Ask these people if they would be open to mentoring you in an informal capacity. Be prepared to discuss what your expectations are for this relationship, along with having a plan of action for how you will manage this process. Yes, I said *you*. When working in an informal mentoring capacity, it is important that you simplify this process for your mentor(s). You must develop, manage, and own it. No exceptions!

What if ... I can't identify a mentor in my company?

Great mentors are everywhere. Don't limit yourself to the workplace. In fact, it is wise to have more than one mentor and, if possible, hear from a variety of voices. In other words, you may seek a particular mentor due to his or her level of success, another due to their background and experiences, and yet another due to their connections and influence. You get the idea. Diversify. You can never have too many mentors. Diversification is key.

Professional Coaching

What if ... I don't know if coaching is right for me?

Start by determining the kind of support you are seeking. If you are looking for someone to assist with the following, then coaching may be a great option.

- ❏ Discovering or clarifying goals
- ❏ Holding you accountable
- ❏ Challenging, stretching, and encouraging you
- ❏ Accelerating results

What if ... my company does not offer professional coaching services?

There are a lot of companies that recognize the value of providing professional coaching services to their employees. However, if your company does not offer this then here are several options available to you: (1) The International Coach Federation (ICF) (www.coachfederation.org) is a great resource for locating and connecting with credentialed coaches. (2) Some colleges/universities provide these services to students through their Career Services Department. (3) Trained coaches who are working toward obtaining professional credentials often seek clients to fulfill their coaching requirements by offering pro bono or discounted services. You can visit the ICF's Career Centre or join any of the online public coaching communities to connect with a prospective coach. Typically, these communities are free to join and are managed by the individual coaching schools. You can obtain a list of accredited/approved schools from the ICF website.

Note to Readers

They often refer to it as just another paycheck. You know who "they" are. They are the people that go to work each day with the mindset of just getting by. They are your coworkers who constantly complain about one day quitting, yet never do. They are the bosses that fail to develop you because they never took the time to develop themselves. They are your friends and family members that dismiss your desire to have a fulfilling and satisfying career because to them that possibility does not exist. *They* may have even been *you* at various times.

There are many people that never give their career a second thought. "It is what it is," they say. Unfortunately, that mindset is the reason why so many people do work that drains and discourages them, or as I like to call it, "cubicle suicide."

This is also the reason why corporations across the country are experiencing a decrease in engagement and high turnover. The problem doesn't lie with the people that are being hired. The problem lies in the work that they are being hired to do. What happened to doing work that you enjoy? What happened to contributing your personal best? What happened to blazing your career?

Settling has become a way of life for many. One by one people give up on their dreams and settle for "what is" instead of "what could be." At the first sign of challenge or opposition, they settle. Many people settle in their personal relationships. They settle in their goals, and more importantly, they settle on who they are. Career mediocrity is an epidemic. One that can steal your joy, purpose and meaning. The time has come to dismiss the naysayers and craft a career that gives you life instead of one that sucks it from you.

Take a look at your career right now. Do you even have one? Are you happy, fulfilled, and inspired? In what areas have you settled? Think about this for a few minutes. Now ask yourself, what do you really want? And don't stop at surface level fluff about how you want to help people or make the world a better place. Dig deeper. Staying on the surface is what average people do. They live their life at a level just above survival yet way below their capabilities. They will never have the courage to journey beyond mediocrity. Not because they are not ready, but because they don't know that they are.

Note to Organizational Leaders

The success of your company depends on your ability to harness and develop the potential of your talent. You must take responsibility for developing those that are under your guidance. And if you want them to perform at their best, you must support their efforts. Stop fixating on numbers and performance metrics. Turn your attention instead to what matters most—your people. Some leaders may not be ready to view their people as anything more than employees who work for pay. However, it's time to create workplace experiences that extend beyond the structures that are currently in place. I challenge you to not only support the path to success for every person who has the opportunity to work for your organization, but to lead it. Serving in this way will undoubtedly change how you view your role as a leader and will ultimately become your greatest accomplishment.

Let's redefine careers in a way that truly reflects our greatest human gift: the ability to serve and support of others.

Be the leader you wanted and needed in your career!

About the Author

Kiana Wilson is the founder of A Sharper U, a career development firm in Tampa, Florida. Although the professional community knows her as an accomplished coach, trainer, educator and speaker, Kiana has walked the same path as many of her clients and knows firsthand the challenges associated with taking professional risks and pursuing career goals.

With an MBA in Management and professional certifications as an Associate Certified Coach, Professional in Human Resources, and Global Career Development Facilitator, Kiana has dedicated over ten years of her career to educating, training, and developing others, both inside and outside the workplace.

Her career development advice has been featured in the publication, *You Are More Accomplished Than You Think,* and her expertise in the fields of coaching and human resources are demonstrated through her HR coaching programs: *Achieving Organizational Excellence Through Personal Mastery* (co-created) and *Coaching Gen Y and Beyond.*

As an adjunct professor, Kiana's love for educating others extends to the classroom where she instructs undergraduate business courses in management, career development, and human resources. A life-long learner herself, Kiana often serves as a mentor to students and colleagues alike.

The proud mother of a teenager and an overly active poodle, Kiana values a healthy work-life balance and spends much of her downtime socializing with friends, traveling, or simply relaxing with a good book or movie.

Connect with Kiana:
Website: www.KianaLWilson.com
Facebook: www.Facebook.com/KianaLWilson

Learn more about A Sharper U:
Website: www.ASharperU.com
Facebook: www.Facebook.com/ASharperUInc
Twitter: www.Twitter.com/ASharperU

A Special Invitation (For You)

I'm always grateful to connect with my readers and learn more about how I can support their success. If you have not already done so, join my community today. Leave a comment, send me your questions, or simply stop by and say hi! I look forward to getting to know you and adding even more value to your career. Thank you so much for your support!

Join My Community
- Connect with me on Facebook.
    - Go to www.Facebook.com/KianaLWilson
    - Like my page
    - Invite friends and family
- Sign up for my career development newsletter.

○ Go to www.KianaLWilson.com/Resources or scan the QR code below.

Spread the Word

- Use the **#2Sharp2Fail** hashtag.
  ○ Facebook
  ○ Twitter
  ○ LinkedIn
  ○ Instagram
- Start an online discussion.
  ○ Write a blog
  ○ Moderate a social media thread
  ○ Create and share text images with your favorite
  ○ *Too Sharp to Fail* quotes
- Purchase copies for friends and family.
  ○ Birthdays
  ○ Graduations
  ○ Book Clubs
  ○ Just because

A free eBook edition is available with the purchase of this book.

To claim your free eBook edition:

1. Download the Shelfie app.
2. Write your name in upper case in the box.
3. Use the Shelfie app to submit a photo.
4. Download your eBook to any device.

Shelfie

A **free** eBook edition is available
with the purchase of this print book.

CLEARLY PRINT YOUR NAME ABOVE IN UPPER CASE

Instructions to claim your free eBook edition:
1. Download the Shelfie app for Android or iOS
2. Write your name in **UPPER CASE** above
3. Use the Shelfie app to submit a photo
4. Download your eBook to any device

Print & Digital Together Forever.

Snap a photo

Free eBook

Read anywhere

CPSIA information can be obtained
at www.ICGtesting.com
Printed in the USA
BVOW06235603031 7
4777618V00001B/1/P

3119202119 7544